The BRAMBLY HEDGE

MUSIC BOOK

Simple tunes for small
mice and children
inspired by Jill Barklem's
Brambly Hedge books

MUSIC BY PHILIP STOTT
ILLUSTRATED BY JILL BARKLEM

COLLINS

First published by HarperCollins 1991

Text and illustrations copyright © Jill Barklem
1980, 1983, 1984, 1986, 1988, 1990
Music and instructions copyright © Philip Stott 1991
Volume copyright © HarperCollins 1991

ISBN 0 00 184087 6

This book is set in 13/16
Stempel Garamond Roman

Printed and bound in Hong Kong

CONTENTS

INTRODUCTION

THIS BOOK IS FOR ...

Small mice and children who have started to learn the descant (soprano) recorder at school or at home and who are looking for enjoyable music to play by themselves or with their friends. The pieces may also be played for fun on any suitable musical instrument, from a piano to a violin.

The musical notes used are strictly limited to the nine easiest on the descant (soprano) recorder, from D above written Middle C to C one octave above, including F sharp and B flat. The first piece, Wilfred's 'ABC', has been specially written to help children practise these notes, and there is a page of Brambly Hedge 'Musical Notes' showing the fingering patterns for each.

All the music is inspired by Jill Barklem's famous books about Brambly Hedge, which lies on the other side of the stream across the field. This is the home of the mice of Brambly Hedge, who like to sing and dance, play pipes and fiddles, and for whom this simple music was first written. I hope you enjoy it just as much, and I know that you will love Jill Barklem's drawings of life amongst the tangled roots and stems of this secret world.

PHILIP STOTT
Winter, 1990

BRAMBLY HEDGE 'MUSICAL NOTES'

Here is Wilfred's *FINGERING CHART* for every note in *The Brambly Hedge Music Book*. There are nine notes in all, from D to C, including F sharp and B flat. The fingering patterns shown are for the descant (soprano) recorder. You should practise them in order very carefully to make sure that you remember all the patterns perfectly before going on to try the pieces. If you forget how to play a note, turn back to this page to check the correct finger pattern.

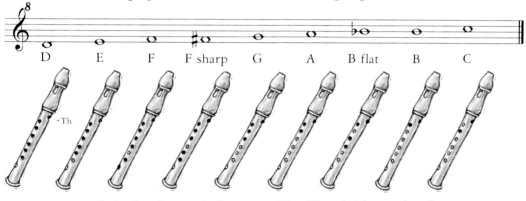

● = hole closed   ○ = hole open   Th = Thumb (always closed)

SOME IMPORTANT MUSICAL SIGNS

A *breathing mark*: take a breath at the places indicated by this sign.

A *slur*: only tongue the first note letting the other notes follow smoothly on.

Staccato: a dot over or under a note means that the note must be played short and detached; tongue 'dot' for staccato notes.

A note with a dash over or under it should be slightly stressed.

An *accent* sign: such notes should be strongly stressed.

A *pause*: you can linger on this note longer than usual.

~1~
WILFRED'S 'ABC'
(for practising)

For his birthday, Wilfred Toadflax received a lovely new whistle (you can see it in the picture). After many squeaks and wrong notes, Mr Apple, who lived next door, told his kindly wife that Wilfred clearly needed lessons from the blackbird. Here is one of those important lessons.

Wilfred's 'ABC' contains all the notes you will meet in this book. If you practise it, very slowly at first, until you can play it steadily without any squeaks or wrong notes, you will then have no problems playing the pieces which follow.

NOTE
By the way, this little sign (⌢) tells you where to take a breath. mf *means you should play the music moderately loud.*

REMEMBER - IF YOU HAVE FORGOTTEN HOW TO PLAY A NOTE, TURN BACK TO PAGE 5.

Steadily and without too many squeaks

Now prac - tise all your Cs and Gs, with

A and E and G (ag - ain!), Then D comes next and

F you see, with B B C, so ea - sy! But

B - flat makes us ra - ther sad, though F - sharp makes us

hap - py, So learn with Wil - fred how to play, the *louder*

sim - ple scale for 'mou - ses!'

~2~
'HERE WE COME TO GATHER NUTS'

Wilfred could not spend all his time playing music, however. In *Autumn Story*, the mice had to work very hard gathering in stores for the winter. Every morning they went out to collect seeds, berries, nuts and roots, which they took back to the Store Stump. This is the happy song they sang while they worked together in the fields and the hedgerows.

NOTE
The music should be played briskly (quite quickly) because the weather is chilly. f means loud and mp moderately soft. Also remember to breathe in the right places, where there is a breathing sign (⌢) or a rest.

Briskly (it is autumn!)

'Here we come to gather nuts,

Hips and haws and a - corn cups!'

9

~3~
'HICKORY, DICKORY, DANDELION CLOCK'

Wilfred sometimes tries to avoid work, and when he isn't being naughty with his catapult (see the picture), he likes to play the tune he performed at his Birthday Party, 'Hickory, Dickory, Dandelion Clock.'

To play this properly, you will need to collect a dandelion clock with all its parachute seeds attached. Where the music says, 'Blow!' (the special notes looking like this: ♩), you must quickly stop playing your recorder, and try to 'puff' away the dandelion seeds, but always in time to the music, and doing your best to sound the written notes. I wonder if you will blow away all the seeds by the end of the tune, which gives you three last 'puffs' just before the final note.

NOTE
If you can't find a dandelion clock, you should try to use something else, like pieces of thread, cotton wool, confetti (from Poppy's wedding), or paper models. If you are now as good as Wilfred became on his whistle, you should be able to play 'Hickory, Dickory, Dandelion Clock' without any squeaks at all.

Steadily and *no* squeaks

'Hic-ko-ry, Dic-ko-ry, Dan-de-lion Clock'

Puffily

'Blow, blow, blow!'— 'Blow, blow, blow!'—

mp smoothly

'Blow, blow, blow!'— 'Blow, blow,

blow!'— *mp getting louder*

'Puff, puff, puff!' 'Tea-time!'

~4~
LULLABY FOR PRIMROSE

Working hard collecting blackberries or getting lost and having big adventures can make a small mouse very tired. This is the Lullaby (song to put a child to sleep) which Lady Woodmouse sang to Primrose after her daughter had become lost in the brambles and briars one dark autumn evening. Luckily, Mr Apple and his friends found her, and brought her back home to a mug of hot acorn coffee and a safe, comfy bed.

NOTE
You should play a lullaby quietly and tenderly. pp means very soft, and two notes have pause signs (⌢) over them, which means that you can play these notes a little longer than usual, to suit your own taste.

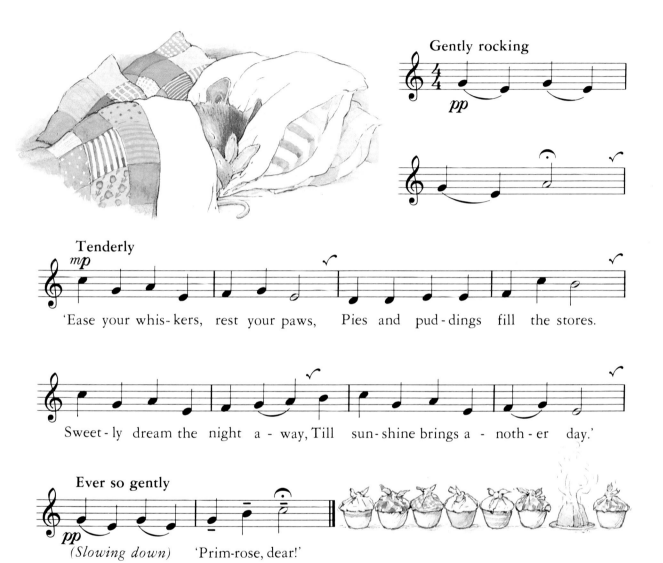

Gently rocking

pp

Tenderly
mp

'Ease your whis-kers, rest your paws,   Pies and pud-dings fill the stores.

Sweet-ly dream the night a - way, Till   sun-shine brings a - noth-er day.'

Ever so gently
pp
(Slowing down)   'Prim-rose, dear!'

13

~5~

WATER WHEELS

I wonder what it is like going to sleep to the sound of water wheels? There are two large wheels working by Brambly Hedge stream, one for the dairy mill, looked after by Poppy Eyebright, and one for Dusty Dogwood's flour mill.

In this piece, you must start the wheels going, at first quite slowly, and then faster and faster.

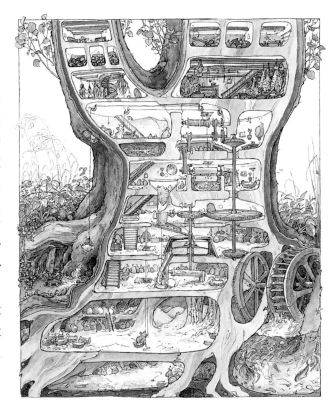

NOTE

Many notes in Water Wheels must be played **staccato**, *that is, short and detached. Such notes have a dot over or under them, (like this: ♪, ♩).*
To play notes staccato, *you should tongue the word, 'dot'.*

Not too fast

mf

Faster

And faster

softer _

louder _

15

~6~

'RING THE BELLS FOR POPPY'

Miss Poppy Eyebright and Mr Dusty Dogwood were married by the stream on a beautiful Midsummer's Day. This is the music that was specially written by the Old Vole for Poppy's wedding.

NOTE
Although you can play Poppy's music on your own, it is much better to perform it with a friend, who should ring a small bell where shown. On the last note, the ᴛʀ‑‑‑‑‑ *means that the bell should be jingled for the full length of the note.*

Joyfully

Bells

'Ring the bells for Pop-py!'

louder _ _ _ _ _ _ *f*

17

~7~
EVENSONG

Early evening in high summer or early autumn is a magical time in the Hedge, the woods and the surrounding fields. Dusk falls, golden and misty; the music captures the feel of this very special time of day.

NOTE

A piece like this is called an 'Idyll', which is music that recalls the peace and quiet of the countryside. You should play it very smoothly, and with a lot of feeling. Remember the pause on the final note.

With mystery

mp

smoothly

louder _ _ _ _ _ _ _ _

_ _ _ _ _ _ _ mf

quieter _ _ _ _ _ _ _ _

slower and softer _ _ _ _ _ _ _ _ _ _

~8~
THE WEAVERS' TUNE

As the year moves on into late autumn and winter, the mice of Brambly Hedge stay more indoors, working at their spinning and weaving. Houses become filled with the *Whirr, whirr!* of spinning wheels, and the *Clickety, clack!* of the loom.

NOTE
This music captures the sounds of spinning and weaving. It is best played with a friend, who should make the Clickety, clack! *sounds by striking together two wooden sticks or spoons as marked. The music should be very regular, like a machine.*

Like a machine

Wooden sticks *or* spoons

Clic – ke – ty, Clack!   Clic – ke – ty Clack!

Whirr, whirr!

louder _ _ _ _ _ _ _ _ *f*

louder _ _ _ _ _ _ _ _ _ _ _ _

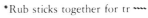

*Rub sticks together for tr 〰

~9~

MY LORD WOODMOUSE'S JIG

Whatever the occasion, whether a summer wedding or a winter Snow Ball, the mice of Brambly Hedge love to dance. This is one of their very favourite dances, a fast and twirly jig named in honour of Lord Woodmouse, who lives in the Old Oak Palace in the middle of the Hedge (you can see his best bedroom in the picture).

NOTE

A jig is a lively jumping dance. Basil, the keeper of the hedgerow wines, is particularly famous for his jigs. This one gets faster and louder towards the end; ff means very loud, but do not overblow and squeak horribly so as to frighten Primrose!

~10~
'WHEN THE DAYS ARE THE DARKEST'

This was the verse so dramatically performed by Primrose and Wilfred on Midwinter's Eve – you will remember that they threw off their cloaks and donned their old hats with a flourish at the words, 'The promise of SPRING!' Such songs, performed before roaring log fires, are much loved in the dark depths of snowy winter.

NOTE
Although the key signature of this piece demands an E flat, there is no need to worry, because Lord Woodmouse has cleverly managed to avoid writing any E flat notes at all – so you will not have to play one! But you must note that the key signature changes halfway through the music to mark the move from winter (dark) to spring (happy). In the first half, there are B flats; in the second part, there are no B flats, but F sharps instead. p means soft.

Darkly

p

"When the days are the short-est, the nights are the cold-est, The frost is the sharp-est, the year is the old-est, The sun is the weak-est, the wind is the hard-est, The snow is the deep-est, the skies are the dark-est, So

(gradually slower) _ _ _ _ _ _

Happily

po-lish your whis-kers and ti-dy your nest, And_ dress in your rich-est and fin-est and best... For win-ter has brought you the worst it can bring, And_ now it will

(Louder and louder!) _ _ _ _ _

give you The prom-ise of SPRING!'

~11~
'ROAST THE CHESTNUTS'
A Round

In the depth of winter, whenever the mice of Brambly Hedge gather together by the hearth for a celebration, they will sing one of their favourite rounds. A 'round' is a short, but continuous piece of music, in which each voice enters in turn, usually with the same tune

at the same pitch, just like 'Frère Jacques'. 'Roast the Chestnuts' is especially popular when sung with great vigour by Mr Apple, Dusty Dogwood, Basil and Lord Woodmouse, who always start in that order. It is also the special round sung every year when the mice haul in the Midwinter log.

NOTE

Although you can play the tune on your own (follow Mr Apple's line), it is best to play this piece properly as a round, just as Mr Apple and his three friends do. To finish you can do one of two things:

1. end all together by playing the last two bars and the note with a pause sign over it; or

2. end one by one in the order marked in the music (1 to 4), first Mr Apple (1), then Dusty Dogwood (2), followed by Basil (3), and, last of all, Lord Woodmouse (4).

You can, of course, go on as long as you want to by repeating the music between the repeat marks:

warm as toast in - side to -night.'
[*Final time* **f**]

[*Final time* **f**]

[*Final time* **f**]

'Roast the chest-nuts, etc.'
mf [*Final time* **f**]

Louder and slower_____ff

Louder and slower_____ff

Louder and slower_____ff

Louder and slower_____ff

~12~
SWEET DREAMS

I suspect you are very tired now after playing all this music! The Toadflax children, Catkin, Clover, Teasel and Wilfred, love the snow, and music, and dancing, but they, too, eventually become drowsy and need their beds. This is a lullaby for them, and our farewell to Brambly Hedge, where every mouse will soon be fast asleep and the lights dimmed in tree and stump.

NOTE
This little piece contains many slurred notes, because it should be played very smoothly. A slur is a curved line linking two or more notes of a different pitch, like this:

You play the slur by tonguing only the first note and then letting the others follow smoothly on. Be mouse quiet throughout. Shhh!

Mouse quiet

p *gently*

pp *slower*_____